Grasshoppers

Edited by Heather C. Hudak

Published by Weigl Publishers Inc.
350 5th Avenue, Suite 3304, PMB 6G
New York, NY 10118-0069
Website: www.weigl.com

Library of Congress Cataloging-in-Publication Data

Grasshoppers : world of wonder / edited by Heather C. Hudak.
    p. cm.
 Includes index.
 ISBN 978-1-59036-870-1 (hard cover : alk. paper) -- ISBN 978-1-59036-871-8 (soft cover : alk. paper)
 1. Grasshoppers--Juvenile literature. I. Hudak, Heather C., 1975-
 QL508.A2G743 2009
 595.7'26--dc22

                              2008023853

Printed in the United States of America
1 2 3 4 5 6 7 8 9 0 12 11 10 09 08

Editor: Heather C. Hudak
Design: Terry Paulhus

Weigl acknowledges Getty Images as its primary image supplier.

CONTENTS

What is a Grasshopper?

Have you ever seen an insect that can jump from one end of the room to another in one leap? The grasshopper is an insect that can hop, walk, and fly. There are more than 20,000 types of grasshopper on Earth.

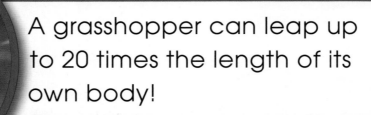

A grasshopper can leap up to 20 times the length of its own body!

5

Back in Time

Grasshoppers first lived during the time of the dinosaurs. This was about 75 million years ago!

Even after all of the dinosaurs died, grasshoppers continued to live. They developed and changed over time.

Grasshopper Life Cycle

A female grasshopper lays 300 eggs on plant roots. Then, she forms a **pod** around them. The eggs hatch into nymphs.

Nymphs look much like adult grasshoppers, except they are white. After they have been in sunlight, nymphs get the colors and markings of an adult. Nymphs **shed** their skin many times in the process of becoming adults.

Nymph

Adult

What Does a Grasshopper Look Like?

How many parts do you have in your body? Grasshoppers have three main parts. These are the head, thorax, and abdomen. Grasshoppers have six legs, four wings, and two **antennae**. Their body is covered with a hard shell called an exoskeleton.

Grasshoppers can grow up to 4.3 inches (11 centimeters) long. This is the same length as a bicycle pedal.

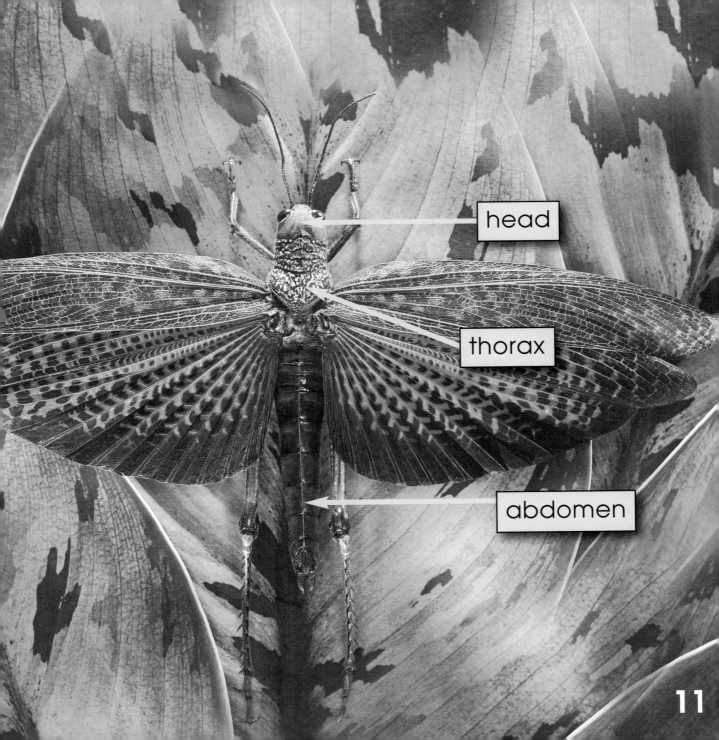

head

thorax

abdomen

Family Fun

How big is your family? Is it small or large? Some grasshoppers live in groups called clouds. These groups are made up of five or more grasshoppers. Other grasshoppers, called locusts, live in **swarms**.

Sometimes, locusts destroy crops.

The Flying Musician

Grasshoppers have two pairs of wings. The front wings act as hard covers for the hind wings. The hind wings are used to fly.

Some grasshoppers rub their wings together to make music. Others rub their back legs across their front wings or snap their wings together while flying. This makes a "chirping" sound.

What's for Dinner?

Do you like to eat meat, or do you prefer vegetables? Grasshoppers are herbivores. This means that they eat plants.

Grasshoppers eat any plants they can find easily. They may eat green grass in a lawn or even carrots from a garden.

Grasshoppers use their short front legs to hold **prey** and to walk. Their long back legs are used for hopping.

Home Sweet Home

Grasshoppers live in warm places all over the world. They usually live among small plants that grow near the ground. Some also live near swamps.

Most grasshoppers live in dry places that have plenty of grass.

Insect Lore

There are many stories about grasshoppers around the world. Some people believe that, if they find a brown grasshopper in their house, they will find money. If they find a green grasshopper, they will lose money.

Others believe that, if there is a grasshopper in their house, an important person is about to visit.

Draw a Grasshopper

Supplies
A white piece of paper, a sharp pencil, and an eraser

1. To start, draw a large oval on the sheet of paper. This is the grasshopper's body. Then, draw two smaller, narrow ovals at the back of the large oval.

2. Next, draw the lines on the head. Add a mouth and an eye. Then, add wings just behind the grasshopper's head.

3. Draw the back legs by starting in the middle of the body. There are six pairs of legs.

4. Next, color the grasshopper. Most grasshoppers are green, but you may choose any color you like.

Find Out More

To learn more about grasshoppers, visit these websites.

Grasshopper Fact Page
http://insected.arizona.
edu/ghopperinfo.htm

Grasshopper
www.enchantedlearning.
com/paint/subjects/
insects/orthoptera/
Grasshopperprintout.shtml

BioKids
www.biokids.umich.edu/
critters/Acrididae

FEATURE SITE:
http://ipm.ncsu.edu/
AG271/small_grains/
grasshoppers.html

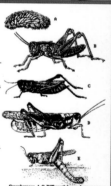

Grasshoppers

Differential grasshopper, *Melanoplus differentialis* (Thomas);
Twostriped grasshopper, *Melanoplus bivittatus* (Say);
Redlegged grasshopper, *Melanoplus femurrubrum* (De Geer)
Acrididae, ORTHOPTERA

DESCRIPTION (several species)

Adult - Fully grown grasshoppers range in length from 19 to 38 mm. Coloration varies with species. Redlegged grasshoppers are reddish brown with a yellow underside. The differential grasshopper is basically brownish yellow or olive green with contrasting black markings on the hindlegs which distinctively resemble chevrons. Greenish yellow in color, the twostriped grasshopper has two pale stripes running down its back from the head to the wing tips. Color plate.

Egg - Egg pods are oval to elongate and often curved. Often the size of kernels of rice, eggs may be white, yellow-green, tan or various shades of brown depending on the species.

Nymph - Nymphs resemble small, wingless adults. Newly hatched nymphs are white; however, after exposure to sunlight, they assume the distinctive colors and markings of adults.

BIOLOGY

Distribution - Grasshoppers occur throughout the continental United States. Extensive grasshopper damage to crops, however, is fairly restricted to subhumid, semiarid areas which receive 25.4 to 76.2 cm (about 10 to 30 inches) of rain annually. Such an area includes the states from Montana and Minnesota, southward into New Mexico and Texas. Although common in North Carolina, grasshoppers seldom pose a severe threat to crops in this state.

Host Plants - These three species of grasshoppers are general feeders which attack many kinds of plants. They are known to cause losses in small grains, corn, alfalfa, soybeans, cotton, clover, grasses, and tobacco.

Damage - Although approximately 600 species of grasshoppers occur in the United States, the 3 species covered in this note are the damaging species most likely to be found in North Carolina. Grasshoppers rarely damage the commercially valuable parts of crop plants. They occasionally cause injury to small grains by feeding on stems, causing heads of grain to be snipped off. The most common damage in North Carolina occurs to forages and around the margins of corn and tobacco fields. Color plate.

Life History - Economically important grasshoppers overwinter as eggs in the soil. Eggs hatch throughout April, May and June as soil temperatures rise and spring rains begin. The first nymph to hatch out of the egg pod leaves a tunnel from the pod to the soil surface, making emergence easier for the nymphs which follow. Nymphs feed and grow for 35 to 50 days, molting five or six times during this period. Development proceeds most rapidly when the weather is warm and not too wet.

Two weeks after mating, females begin to deposit clusters of eggs in the soil. During the process, a glue-like secretion cements soil particles around the egg mass forming a protective "pod." Each pod may contain 15 to 150 eggs depending on the species of grasshopper which laid them. Under optimum conditions, each female produces 300 eggs. Generally, agriculturally important grasshoppers produce only one generation per year. Redlegged grasshoppers, however, have two generations per year plus a partial third in Florida.

Grasshoppers. A-C, Differential grasshopper egg, nymph, and adult. D, Redlegged grasshopper adult. E, Twostriped grasshopper adult laying eggs.

Glossary

antennae: long, thin body parts that extend from an insect's head

pod: a pouch

prey: an animal that is hunted by another animal for food

shed: to come off, to be replaced by another growing underneath

swarms: large groups

Index